Florida
GOD BLESS FLORIDA

Florida

Flor

Florida

Florida

FLOR

Florida

Florida

FLORIDA
MIAMI
TAMPA
JACKSONVILLE
ORLANDO

Florida

Florida

Florida

flor
ida!

Florida

Florida

POLICE

FLORIDA
1$
Florida
special edition

Florid

Florida

Florida

Florida
RUM

Florida

Florida

FLORIDA

BEER
Florida

Florida
Beer

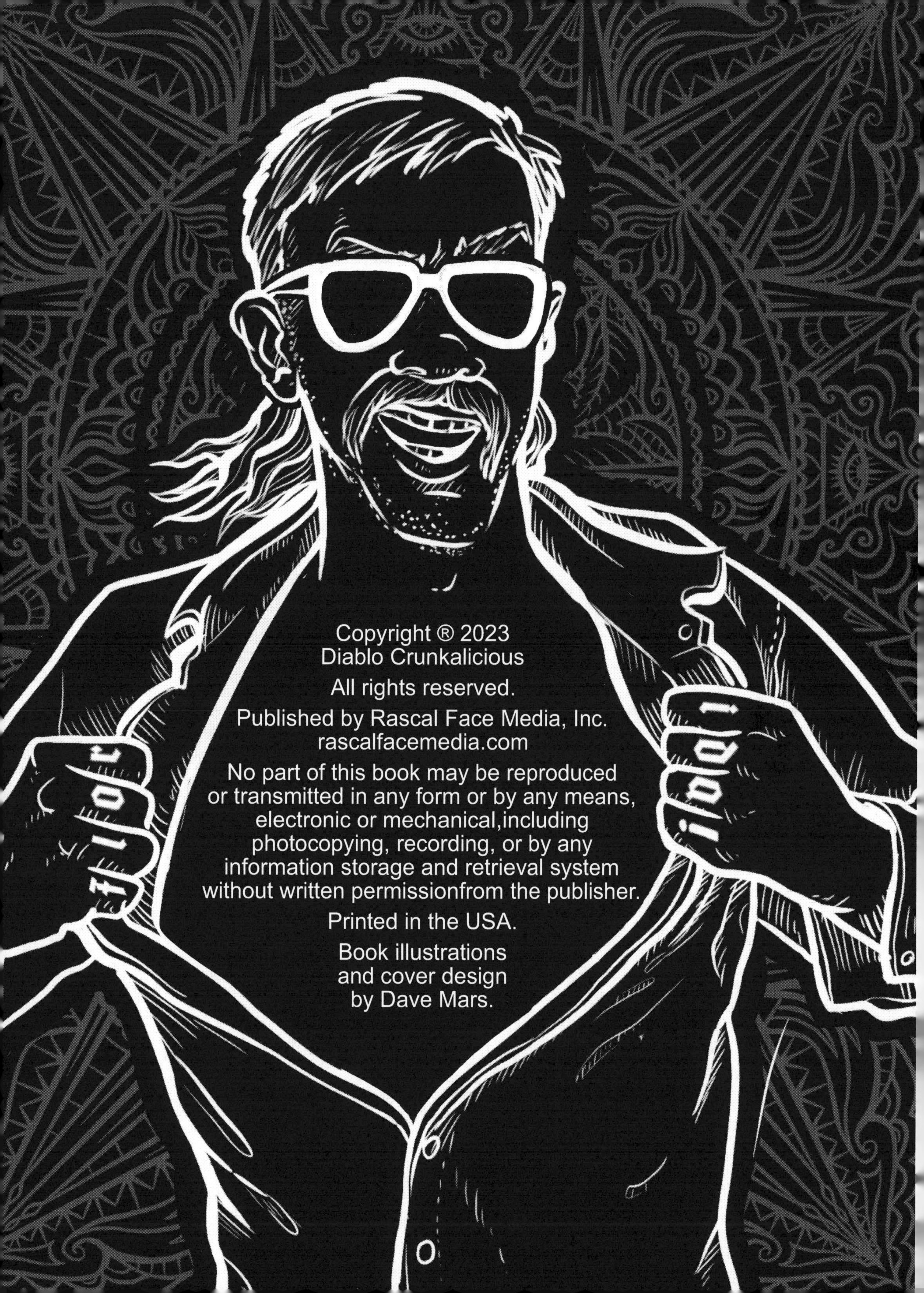

Published by Rascal Face Media, Inc.
rascalfacemedia.com

Printed in the USA.

Book illustrations and cover design by Dave Mars.

Made in United States
Orlando, FL
12 December 2023

40693376R00039